With the
compliments
of the
Canada Council

Avec les
hommages
du Conseil des
Arts du Canada

3/16/77

COMPLETE
POEMS OF
SAINT DENYS
GARNEAU

◄◄◄►►►

Translated

With an Introduction

By

JOHN GLASSCO

Translated from *Poésies complètes* (Fides, 1949) by permission of the Corporation des Editions Fides

Library of Congress Catalogue Card No. 75-1984

ISBN 0 88750 153 2

Book design by Michael Macklem

Printed in Canada

PUBLISHED IN CANADA BY OBERON PRESS

INTRODUCTION

I

Today, 30 years after his death, Saint-Denys-Garneau still shares with Emile Nelligan the first place in the poetry of French Canada. The similarity of their careers—the almost overnight flowering of creativity, and its no less sudden withering away—is coincidental, and the two have nothing in common beyond being a good deal more than merely "poets of Quebec"; and they are in fact the only poets of their nation whose accomplishment transcends nationality. But Nelligan marks the culmination of a trend: his work stands as the high-water mark of French-Canadian romanticism; while Saint-Denys-Garneau initiates a new era of both sensibility and prosody, and invokes and announces the future.

This is not to overlook the cultural importance of the third major poet of Quebec, Alain Grandbois, whom contemporary French-Canadian poets have chosen to follow on the path of an eloquence verging on fustian, a sensibility approaching sentimentality and a magnificent rejection of ideas. But while Grandbois is the poet of the splendours of the Word, who has almost singlehandedly freed French-Canadian poetry from what has been called "the prison of the self-regarding self," Saint-Denys-Garneau is still the poet of the Idea, who has plumbed the depths of consciousness and conscience alike, and in doing so has, I believe, raised for himself a more lasting monument. As theoreticians of the art of poetry itself, they can of course sustain no contest: one has only to compare the luminous insights that stud Saint-Denys-Garneau's *Journal* with the civilized clichés of Grandbois in *Avant le chaos* and in his occasional contributions to periodicals. Their views of poetry are in fact as divergent as their practice. Both, as true poets, are spokesmen of an individual suffering and joy; but while Grandbois' ecstasy and anguish are of the flesh and the affections, Saint-Denys-Garneau's are of the soul and the intellect.

Of these three outstanding names in French-Canadian poetry, then—to which one must add those of Paul Morin, Robert Choquette and Alfred DesRochers, none of whom however, like Nelligan, has had any influence on the contemporary poetry of Quebec—Saint-Denys-Garneau remains the one who seems worthiest of a translation into English of his entire mature poetic output.

The translation of poetry, as I noted in the Introduction to the *Poetry of French Canada in Translation* (1970), is often decried, mainly on the grounds alleged by Robert Frost, that "what gets lost is the poetry itself." This allegation is simply not true: Northrop Frye has even gone so far as to say it is the opposite of the truth. But let us look at the facts. The best poetry has always reached its widest audience through the medium of translation, and its various messages—though inevitably lacking the original music and verbal magic—have come through, the skeletons of its forms and movement are retained, the ideas and images that are its lifeblood are transmitted. "The massy trunk of sentiment," as Dr. Johnson says, "is safe by its solidity, but the blossoms of elocution easily drop away." And since faithful translation would thus seem a kind of test and ultimate screening of all poetry—how else have the good poets managed to survive?—we must conclude that any poem that dies under the hands of the most skilful and sympathetic translator has a prime constitutional defect, and that the poets who rely on verbal hermetics, apocalyptic surprises, typographical innovations and simple sonorities (to the neglect of those essentials of form and meaning which transcend language and are, as it were, the universals of human communication) must resign themselves to cultivating a provincial garden—as indeed so many of the contemporary poets of Quebec seem content to do. Such qualities of *le restrictif*, which Saint-Denys-Garneau condemned in his *Journal*, have no place in his own poetry, any more than in that of Nelligan or Grandbois; and this common rejection of parochialism—one might call it *québecisme*—is what situates them in the mainstream of poetry, not as poets of Quebec but of the world.

It is some 35 years since Msgr. Camille Roy dismissed the poetry of Saint-Denys-Garneau as a "collection of poems in the style of Valéry—that is to say, more or less incomprehensible." "In these poems [he goes on] there is undoubtedly an attempt, however laboured, either at introspection or at the interpretation of the external. But this attempt all too often results in unintelligibility. For some readers, the hermetic partakes of the sublime. Here, the sublime is too closely veiled. *L'esprit français* will never lend itself to a thought it cannot perceive—the poet having hidden it under the bushel of an overly obscure symbolism. Moreover Monsieur Garneau writes without periods or commas." Roy seems to have missed the point entirely. Or has he? By his lights, this poetry was not "poetry" at all; and indeed it was not the voice of a Pamphile Lemay, a Chapman or a Nérée Beauchemin, the French-Canadian poets especially prized by this learned disciple of Brunetière. His verdict is nonetheless important, because it points up Saint-Denys-Garneau's definitive break with the past and with the worn-out body of French-Canadian literature which Roy supported with such

7

eloquence and erudition; it marks a meeting of minds and epochs, and even raises the question of just what constitutes *l'esprit français*—something, we must note in passing, quite different from the still undetermined *esprit québecois*, which was admittedly the concern of neither writer. This "French spirit," we can see now, was in fact magnificently exemplified by Saint-Denys-Garneau—by his search for new symbols and formulas of expression, his clarity of thought and command of nuance and the absolute sincerity and painstaking of his art.

As for his place in Quebec literary history, the distinguished French critic Samuel de Sacy has announced flatly, "Insofar as any poetic tradition exists in French Canada, modern poetry, properly considered, begins with Saint-Denys-Garneau. . . . He knew not only the experience of solitude, but solitude felt as something irremediable, as a fatality, a curse, an ineluctable destiny. Thus, by assuming the whole burden of the sentence, he brought salvation to a whole generation of youth and exposed, in his poetry, its feeling of being hunted, abandoned, scorned, divided against itself and reduced to helplessness. By speaking, he exorcised."

This was written in 1958. The generation whose demons he "exorcised" has now matured, and the succeeding wave of young Quebec writers have other demons, much more tangible, to fill the void and to minister to the constant need for something absolute, simple, authoritative and maternal, which is at once the spur and the crutch of *l'esprit québecois*. Mother Church has, for them, been replaced by Mother Quebec, by the incandescent ideal of an exploited and beleaguered land. In such a climate the tormented, inward-looking poetry of Saint-Denys-Garneau is now found to be unsympathetic, outmoded, almost impertinent; moreover, the cool intelligence of the "Notes on Nationalism" in his *Journal* is unacceptable to the advocates of separatism. This has inevitably led to a certain downgrading of his poetry and to a revaluation of his poetic stature, both of which are to some extent justified.

For Saint-Denys-Garneau is not a *great* poet. The very idea of being so "placed" would have horrified him. And his was no false modesty. He knew his limitations: his prophecy of the arrival of *"le créateur, le poète qui donnera au peuple canadien-français son image"* and who will appear "in his own good time," proves that he never thought of casting himself in such a role. It is even doubtful if he saw himself as a French-Canadian poet at all, if indeed he did not hold himself superior to the very spirit of French-Canadian poetry, or at least hold aloof from it. "I need hardly say," his friend Jean Le Moyne tells us, "that he saw our Canadian rhymesters for what they are: exactly nothing." His attitude was in this respect characteristically exclusive and fastidious; more important, his anguish was not localized in any sense of a vulgar emotional *dépaysement*, as in a Hertel or a Miron, but in that of the universal human being.

In fact, this habit of negation had always been one of his greatest strengths. His early ability to *discard* literary influences—Maeterlinck, Henri de Regnier, Claudel—is notable. As Roland Bourneuf has pointed out, he did not read widely, doubtless following the practice of those poets who see in their own suggestibility the greatest danger to their vision and their art. His utter rejection of the fashionable surrealism of his day indicates also the sureness of his taste: the method had nothing to offer him. He was looking always inward, forging his style out of his *entrailles*, pushing back his own horizon, always exploiting his originality, to which was tragically joined the sense of his solitude. From his study of Ramuz he had grasped the principle of an absolute and rigorous sincerity: "to be simply oneself in order to be more than oneself."

9

Hector de Saint-Denys Garneau was born in Montreal on 13 June, 1912, of an old and prominent French-Canadian family. Through his mother he was connected with the Juchereau-Duchesnays, one of whom was granted a seigneury in recompense for military action during the siege of Quebec by Phipps in 1690; through his father he was descended from the historian François-Xavier Garneau and related to the poet Alfred Garneau. His parents lived in Montreal, but had also purchased the seigneurial manor of the Juchereau-Duchesnays at Sainte-Catherine-de-Fossambault near Quebec, where the poet took refuge more and more frequently as his difficulty in communicating with the world increased.

He began to write at an early age, and also to paint. From 1924 to 1927 he attended classes at the Ecole des Beaux Arts in Montreal, but had to discontinue them due to the pressure of his studies, though he did not stop painting. At school—or rather at several schools, for his instability led to frequent changes—he versified with zest and facility in the intervals of making fun of his teachers. He was then a handsome youth, full of gaiety and self-assurance, and frequently possessed by fits of an almost Dionysian ecstasy. But a few of his juvenile poems, written between 1929 and 1933, anticipated the sombre themes of his future work. For in 1928 he had suffered the heart injury which forced him to abandon his studies altogether in 1934 and was to be the immediate cause of his death some ten years later.

Thus, at the age of 22, he was brought face to face with his own imminent death; and the next nine years of his life —the last nine—were passed in intimate converse with a few close friends and in the feverish search for the religious certainty and the poetic "truth" that had always obsessed him. He had abandoned his studies without any hope of ever resuming them, and now had no outside occupation to distract him from his quest. For a year or two he led, outwardly at least, the life of a rich and idle young-man-about-town; but he was already devising and refining his methods of poetic composition, and in August of 1935 produced his first original poems, the "Esquisses en plein air" of his first and only book of poems.

Two years later, in 1937, he underwent the most devastating experience of his life—the publication of this book, the now famous *Regards et jeux dans l'espace*. No sooner had he seen the work in print than he was stricken with horror: he felt he had "exposed" himself in a manner so much at variance with his natural reserve, his shrinking from all display, that he suffered a nervous breakdown. He had, as he tells us in the *Journal*, the sensation of having actually violated and soiled himself. It did not matter that the book went almost unnoticed, and that the few reviews were casual and cursory: his neurosis transformed its very appearance into an act of self-betrayal, a terrible *mistake*. However difficult it is to understand his feelings, they were of crucial importance to his literary career. He never published again.

In the same year he left for Europe, accompanied by his close friend Jean Le Moyne. No sooner had he set sail than he became deeply disturbed, and would even have landed at Father Point if Le Moyne had not restrained him. He spent three tormented weeks in France, and then returned home precipitately. His affliction now became for him the only reality: thenceforward he embraced a solitude which his friends found increasingly difficult to break in upon. After 1939 he withdrew entirely to Sainte-Catherine, where he composed the poems and fragments of *Les solitudes*, obviously with no more thought of their publication than of that of the *Journal* itself. He spent two winters alone in Sainte-

Catherine, in 1940 and 1941, and for the next two years lived there altogether, with his parents.

On 24 October, 1943, after a dinner with some friends of the family during which he behaved with especial gaiety, he set out alone by canoe for an island where he had begun to build a cabin. On the way back he suffered a heart attack, reached the shore with great difficulty and made his way to a nearby farmhouse to telephone his parents. But there was no telephone. Some children found him the following day lying dead near the river. He was in his thirty-second year.

It is easy to see how, a generation later, this combination of elitist background, personal attraction, precarious health and premature death, could create a legendary and spurious image of the poet: as a person of noble extraction (an illusion he himself fostered by transmogrifying his name) and as the *jeune seigneur* of the Manoir of Sainte-Catherine, a role that amused him from time to time; the baseless story of his suicide was also part of the legend. But his minor vanities—satirized by Jacques Ferron in *Le ciel de Québec* with typical horseplay and venom—his uneventful life and casual death, are now of little importance: he lives only through his 2000-odd lines of verse, his few essays and his *Journal*, and will continue to live by them despite his own final and characteristically despairing verdict on his single book of poems: "I was parading in borrowed peacock's feathers; I was covering up my tracks, an utter emptiness clothed in brilliancy." His greatest tragedy was perhaps that he did not understand how good he was.

3

In any evaluation of the art of Saint-Denys-Garneau one must never forget that he was equally attracted by the life of religion. He was constantly tossed between the vocations of artist and ascetic, always fearful of his unfitness for either, always terrified both of the world and of hell. Out of this indecision and fear, these *balancements*, this shrinking and immoderate modesty, and out of his sense of the terrible discrepancy between life and art, and of the evanescence of both, he made his poetry. An unflinching moral dichotomist in the strictest Catholic tradition, he would compromise with no aspect of the Devil; yet, fatally attracted by the "evil" which he confronted in his own sexuality, he fell back on what seemed to him the redeeming beauty of human compassion and on the supernatural grace that somehow redeemed the carnal desire (and above all the auto-eroticism) which his ingrained Jansenism rejected and at last stifled. Overriding all these concepts is his stark terror of death and damnation; for him, the existence of a man like himself was only a way-station between nothingness and an eternity of torment, barely relieved by the fleeting beauty of nature and the forbidden ecstasy of carnal love. It was to poetry that he turned for relief. But poetry was for him communication above all things; and his anguish was thus purified by the most exhausting and consummate art, an art which became for him a quasi-religious duty. For the immediate and unrehearsed expression of his suffering he had recourse to his *Journal*, that terrible record of neurosis, guilt and despair.

This is not the place to discuss the *Journal*, except insofar as it illuminates his poetry, nor to inquire how far either of them reflected any but the most harrowing moments of his actual life—which seems indeed to have had many long periods of tranquillity and even a kind of vegetable happiness; for, like most keepers of intimate journals, he tells us nothing—no more, indeed, than Baudelaire—of his moments of joy: these moments were obviously always private, self-sufficient, craving no record. But it was only in the

Journal that his ideas on poetry were clearly set forth.

These ideas are comprised in the notion, originally drawn from his own aesthetic of painting and never relinquished, that the world of apperception is only a *transparency* through which "being," or absolute reality, is grasped by means of the *signes* or symbols which the artist discerns and selects— in painting by his choice of pure colours, and in poetry by his *fresh* invention of images and rhythms. Full justice has already been done by David Hayne to his "forest of symbols" —those symbols of the pruned tree, the bones, the severed head, the man full of holes, the fleshly mask of the face— which revitalized French-Canadian poetry and permanently supplanted the nightingale, church-bell, ploughshare, snowstorm and so on, which had long burdened it. But his astonishing reshaping of poetic rhythms is no less important, and was accomplished by a virtuosity in devising the most daring combinations of line lengths and stresses, by which, alternating the grave with the gay and stateliness with speed, he gave his finished poems the further dimension of the dance. One of his favourite devices was the *pair-impair* rhythm in which he sought to outdo his master Verlaine by contriving a dazzling alternation of trochees and iambs, and so broke down everything that had heretofore stood between a poetic union of sound and sense. He made the lyric dance as well as sing, thus restoring the long-lost unity of the two disciplines and even, as he suggests in his *Journal*, equating poetic expression with that of David dancing before the Ark. Let us take, for example, the poem "Willows," the second to last of the "Esquisses en plein air," which begins with a dozen short, slow, impressionistic lines, then makes a four-line pause—a calculated hesitation—and then suddenly gathers speed and breaks up into a sparkling counterpoint of reversed stresses, anapaests and syllabic pyrotechnics that resembles nothing more than the close of one of Chopin's

14

joyous impromptus. Or look at the long untitled poem, the first in the section *Sans titre*, where for the first two thirds the alternations of lines, ranging in length from a single foot to a classic alexandrine, reproduce the tension and weight of the tormented, breathless utterance of the poem itself, and where the last third opens out into long lines of a regular, continuous, rolling suavity that enhances, like a pavane, the solemnity of an accepted despair. Again, the opening metronomic four-foot beat of the witty *Commencement perpetuel* reproduces to perfection the idea of *counting*, only to be followed by a conscious disordering of that simple initial rhythm, as the man who is counting, rather amusingly, loses his count. But the finest examples of this marriage of rhythm and meaning occur in the famous *Accompagnement*, written in a kind of brilliant dance-step further reinforced by the wry reiteration of the rhyming *joie* and *moi*, and in the still more famous *Cage d'oiseau*, where the desperate point is driven home, as if by the strokes of a hammer, in the recurrence of simple four-foot trochaic couplets with naive nursery-rhymes.

If undue emphasis seems to have been given here to Saint-Denys-Garneau's mastery of rhythms, it is because this may well be his highest and most lasting achievement. When his religious, neurotic and erotic agonies are forgotten, along with his often hysterical self-pity and his *bondieuserie*—that infantile, saccharine religiosity which occasionally disfigures his work—the marvellous prosody which never failed him may survive everything else: the formal *cachet* it imposed on everything he wrote was at any rate his salvation as a poet.

This technical control of image and emotion is however seen in little more than half of the 40-odd poems that he finished and approved. Much of his work, including over half of *Regards et jeux dans l'espace*, he either rightly repu-

15

diated in his *Journal* or left uncompleted in the manuscripts edited after his death by Elie and Le Moyne. And in fact all too many of the poems in *Les solitudes* are simply unrehearsed fragments, sometimes little more than jottings: they are often formless, at times distressingly awkward and incoherent; but there is no doubt they are, both actually and potentially, superior to the work published during his lifetime. It is impossible to appreciate his poetic stature without, for instance, the sections of *Les solitudes* entitled "Pouvoirs de la parole" and "La mort grandissante": these fragments, one might say, he had shored against his ruins in the final self-imposed exile at Sainte-Catherine, and though we must regret they were never brought to completion we may at least be thankful they were not lost along with the many pages of his *Journal* that were destroyed by his mother after his death. These considerations have led me to include in this book every poem, finished or unfinished, that appears in the *Poésies complètes*, thus affording an uninterrupted view of his poetic development from the exquisitely finished two-dimensional impressionism of his earliest work to the profound and sombre canvases, mostly uncompleted, of his final period of reclusion.

Following the rule laid down in my anthology of French-Canadian poetry, I have not reproduced the original texts. My reasons for not doing so remain the same: the translation of poetry should not be made the occasion for a lesson in a second language or a comparison of techniques; it is not a playground for philologists or students of linguistics; and, to quote Johnson once again, "the first excellence of a translator of poetry is that his versions be such as may be read with pleasure by those who do not know the originals." In short, the translated poem must stand by itself, as something existing in its own right. These reasons seem even more cogent when it is a question of presenting the whole output of a single poet.

In translating the poems I have followed a course that was bound to result in the intrusion of my own personality. Such personal colouring, however unwelcome and however resisted, is inevitable: translations are done by men and women, not by machines; and translation is a search for an equivalent, not for a substitute. These renderings are faithful but not literal. In a few instances, especially in the fragments, they are partial re-creations which hew to their originals only in thought, image and rhythm. But in translating the great majority of the poems, above all those which the poet himself finally approved, I have reproduced his verbal patterns, and particularly his rhythms, with the greatest fidelity. In doing so I have not scrupled to steal many lines from earlier translations, since I see no reason why the mutual thievery of poets should be forbidden the translator of poetry. My outstanding victim has been F. R. Scott, whom I have pillaged of at least a dozen individual lines and more than as many isolated phrases, all of them quite beyond improvement.

Acknowledgements are also made to *Canadian Literature*, the *Tamarack Review*, the *Waterloo Review* and to Oxford University Press as publishers of my anthology *The Poetry of French Canada in Translation*, where many of these translations first appeared.

The text of this translation is based on that of the Poésies complètes *edited by Robert Elie and Jean Le Moyne (Montreal: Fides, 1949), and has been collated with that of the original edition of* Regards et jeux dans l'espace *(Montreal: privately printed, 1937) and with that of the definitive* Oeuvres *edited by Jacques Brault and Benoît Lacroix (Montreal: Presses de l'Université de Montréal, 1971).*

REGARDS ET JEUX
DANS L'ESPACE

1. Jeux

I am far from easy sitting on this chair
And the clasp of an armchair is the worst of all
There I am bound to drowse and die.

But let me cross the torrent by the rocks
Pass bounding from one thing to another
I find my buoyant balance between the two
It is there in suspension that I am at rest.

20

THE GAME

Don't bother me I'm terribly busy

A child is busy building a village
It's a town, a county
And who knows
                  By and by the universe.

He is playing

These wooden blocks he is moving around are houses and
    castles
This board stands for a sloping roof   it looks all right
It's quite a job to know where the cardboard road will turn
It could change the bed of the river altogether
Because of the bridge with its fine reflection in the water of
    the carpet
It's easy to have a big tree here
And put a mountain underneath to raise it up.

Pleasure of play! Paradise of liberty!
And whatever you do don't set your foot in the room
You never know what might be in that corner there
Or whether you won't be crushing the dearest invisible
    flower of all

Here is my box of toys
Full of words to make wonderful patterns
To be matched divided married
Now they are evolutions of a dance
And the next moment a bright burst of the laughter
You thought was lost

A light flick of the finger
And the star
That was hanging carelessly
At the end of a flimsy thread of light
Falls in the water and makes circles.

Who can dare doubt his love and tenderness
But not a cent's worth of respect for the established order
Nor for politeness and its precious "discipline"
A levity and deportment to shock grown-up people

He arranges words like silly songs
And in his eyes you can read his mischievous delight
At seeing how he is shifting everything around under the
    words
And playing with the mountains
As if he owned them.
He turns the room upside down till you don't know where
    you are
As if it were fun simply to fool people.

And yet in his left eye while his right is laughing
The weight of another world clings to the leaf of a tree
As if this could be of tremendous importance
Could count as much in his scales
As the Ethiopian war
In England's.

[NOUS NE SOMMES PAS DES COMPTABLES]

We are not book-keepers

Anyone can see a dollar is made of green paper
But who can see through it but a child?
Who like him sees wholly freely through it
Without letting the dollar or its meaning stand in the way
Nor its value of just a dollar?

No, he sees through this shop window thousands of wonder-
    ful toys
And he has no desire to choose among those treasures
Neither the appetite nor the need
Not he
For his eyes are wide enough to possess them all.

23

PICTURE OF THE DANCE

My children you are dancing badly
True, it is hard to dance here
In this airless place
Here without space which is the heart of the dance.

Not knowing how to play with space
You cannot play within it
Without chains
Poor children who cannot play.
How can you hope to dance? I have seen the walls
The city cutting off your glance before it began
Cropping your maimed vision at the shoulders
Even before one rhythmic movement
Before its race and final rest
Its flowering far beyond the city landscape
Before your glance could flower in marriage with the sky
That wedding of the gaze and sky
Of infinites brought face to face   a clash
Of wonders.

The dance is the second measure and the second flight
It takes possession of the world
After the primal victory
Of the gaze

That gaze which leaves indeed no mark on space
—Less than the bird itself and its wake
Than even the song and its invisible flight
An impalpable shifting of the air—
Itself an insubstantial embrace
Closest of all to the changeless which is the transparent
Like a reflection of the landscape in water
The landscape we never see that falls into the river

So the dance is a paraphrase of the vision
The road recovered that was lost by the searching eyes
A statelier measure slowing to recapture
The all-embracing magic of its beginning.

25

RIVER OF MY EYES

O my eyes this morning, wide as a river
O wave of my eyes swift to reflect all things
And this coolness under my eyelids
A marvel
Circling the images I see

As a stream cools an island
And as the fluent wave curls around
That sun-dappled girl

2. Enfants

Children
Oh the little monsters!

They clasp you around the neck
The way they climb the aspen trees
To make them bend
And pour down over them

They lay their traps
With incredible persistence

They would not leave you alone
Until you were wholly won

Now they have left you
The traitors
        have abandoned you
Laughing as they ran away.

There were some of them who stayed
When the rest went off to play
These remained demurely seated.

There were some who went as far
As the very end of the lane
Their laughter was a thing suspended

All the time they were looking back
just to see if you were watching

A remorse and a regret

But the laughter was not lost
It has taken up its peal
Heard now running in the air
Even though they've disappeared
Where the lane runs down the hill.

30

PORTRAIT

He's a funny child
He's a bird
Now he's gone

You have to find him
Look for him
When he's there

The point is not to frighten him
He's a bird
He's a snail.

He only looks at you to embrace you
Or else he cannot use his eyes

Where to fix them
He plays with them like a countryman with his cap

He must go to meet you
And when he stops
And if he reaches you
He is no longer there

So you must see him coming
And love him while he's on the way.

3. Esquisses en plein air

The voice of the leaves
A song
More clearly   a rustling
Of brighter dresses of the sheerest colours.

34

WATER-COLOUR

Nothing to render you so clearly, fields
And you translucent trees
You leaves
And for your lights, to catch the least of these

Than the water-colour water-clear
Clear gauze this pale veil on the paper.

35

FLUTE

All the fields have sighed through a flute
Fields far as the eye can reach, curled on the hills

All the breath of the fields has found this little green trickle
   of sound for vent
Has found
This green voice almost of the sea
And sighed a limpid sound
                Through a flute.

36

WILLOWS

Their heads inclined
The wind combs the long hair
Of the willows at the water-side
Shakes it out over the water
While they are dreaming
Lost in the vague delight
Of the sun's game among their cold leaves
Or the night's mingling of her sigh with theirs.

37

THE ELMS

In the fields
Calm parasols
Slim, in serene elegance
The elms rise alone or in little family groups.
The calm elms cast a shade
For cows and horses
Standing around them at noon.
They do not speak
I have not heard them sing.
They are artless things
Spreading an airy shade
Quite simply
For the beasts.

38

WILLOWS

The tall willows sing
Tangled with the sky
And their leaves are fountains
In the sky

The wind
Twirls their leaves
Of silver
In the light
And all is a rutilant glitter
And a motion
Flowing
Like waves
You would say the willows were running
Before the wind
And it's the wind
Running in them.

Its eddies in a sky of blue
Flowing around the trunks and limbs
The breeze reversing every leaf
And the light playing around
In a fairyland
Of a thousand reflections
A shimmer of humming-birds
As it dances on the brooks
Dancing
With all its diamonds and its smiles.

PINES AGAINST THE LIGHT

In the light their leafwork is like water
Islands of clear water
On the black of the spruce shadowed against the light

They are all flowing
Each feathery plume, and the spray
An island of bright water at the branch's tip

Each needle a lustre a thread of living water

Each plume a little gushing spring

Running away
Who knows where

They are flowing as I have seen in spring
The willows flowing, the whole tree
Nothing but silver all lustre all a wave
All watery foaming flight
Like the wind made visible
And seeming
A liquid thing
In a magic window.

40

4. Deux paysages

LANDSCAPE IN TWO COLOURS
ON A GROUND OF SKY

Life and death on a pair of hills
A pair of hills and four hillsides
The wildflowers on two sides
The wild shadow on two sides.

The sun upright in the south
Lays his blessing on both peaks
Spreads it over the face of the slopes
Far as the water in the valley
(Looking at all and seeing nothing)

In the valley the sky of water
In the sky of water the water-lilies,
Long stems reach into the deeps
And the sun follows them with a finger
(Follows with a finger, feeling nothing)

On the water rocked by the lilies
On the water pricked by the lilies
On the water pierced by the lilies
Held by a hundred thousand stems
Stand the feet of the pair of hills
One foot flowered with wildflowers
One foot eaten by wild shadow.

And for him who sails in the midst of all
For the fish that leaps in the midst of all
(Seeing a fly at the very most)

Down the slope toward the deeps
Plunge the brows of the pair of hills
One brow of flowers bright in the light
Twenty years' flowers against the sky
And one brow without face or colour
Wanting either sense or sunlight
But wholly eaten by wild shadow
Wholly made of the black the empty
Gap of oblivion—circled by still sky.

44

A dead man calls for a drink
The well is drier than we thought
Who will take the news to the dead man?
The fountain says, My wave is not for him.

See now his handmaidens all in haste
Each with her pitcher to her separate spring
To quench the thirst of the master
A dead man calling for drink.

One of them culls in the depth of the night-blooming garden
The smooth seed welling in the flowers
In the warmth that lasts till the drawing-in of night
And she unfolds this flesh before him

But the dead man is still thirsty and calls for drink.

Another plucks in the silver of moonlit meadows
Corollas closed by the cool of evening
Making a bursting spray
A tender weight sweet to the mouth
And runs to offer it to the master.

But the dead man thirsts and calls for drink.

45

Then the third and foremost of the three sisters
She also runs among the fields
While in the eastern sky swells
The luminous threat of dawn
And she gathers in the net of her gold apron
Sparkling points of morning dew
And fills a cup and offers it to the master

But he is thirsty still and calls for drink.

Then morning breaks in its glory
Spreading light over the valley like a wind
And the dead man made of dust
The dead man pierced like the mist by sunlight
Evaporates and dies
And even his memory has left the earth.

46

5. De gris en plus noir

.

SPLEEN

Oh what a journey we shall take
My soul and I, how long a journey

And what a land we have to see
What a weary land, land of ennui!

Oh to be tired enough at dusk
To turn back and see nothing more

And in the night to die, to die
Of weariness, my soul and I.

49

A SEALED HOUSE

I think of the desolation of winter
Through the long days of solitude
In the dead house—
For a house is dead when nothing is open—
In the sealed house, ringed by the woods

The black woods filled
With bitter wind

In the house clasped by cold
In the desolation of an endless winter

Alone, tending a little fire in a great chimney
Feeding it with dry branches
Piece by piece
To make it last
To stave off the final death of the fire,
Alone with the sadness that can find no vent
That you shut within yourself
And that spreads into the room
Like the smoke of a poor chimney
Drawing badly
When the wind beats on the roof
Puffing the smoke into the room
Until you stifle in the sealed house

Alone with a sadness
Hardly disturbed by the empty fear
That suddenly comes upon you
When the frost snaps the nails in the floor
And the wind makes the woodwork crack

The long nights to keep yourself from freezing
And then with the morning comes the light
More icy than the night.

So, the long months of waiting
For the end of the grasping winter.

I think of the loneliness of winter
Alone
In a sealed house.

51

FEVER

Fire rekindles
Under the ashes

Beware
We do not know
How in the embers

Beware
We know too well
How in the embers
From the faintest breath the fire begins

In the wood's heart
The fire rekindles
Stealthily
From feebleness to force

Beware
The fire rekindles
Scorching the wind as it flies

The fire rekindles
But where can it go
Among the shattered embers
Among dead stumps
Huddled together

The heat is glowing
The wind is burning
The heat is mounting
Blurring the sky

In heavy flashes
The heat is welling
Burning and twisting me

The heat is glowing
But with no clear flame
The heat is rising
But with no bright banner
Blurring the sky
Shaking the trees
Burning the wind as it goes.

The countryside
Pleads for mercy
The cattle stare with frightened eyes
The birds are wild with fear
In the heat-blurred sky

The wind can no longer reach
To where the tall trees
Are stifling
With open arms
For a breath of air

The country pleads for mercy
And the intolerable heat
Of fire rekindled
Among the embers
Has no rift at all
For a single flame
Or for the wind.

6. Faction

PERPETUAL BEGINNING

A man of undetermined age
Rather young and rather old
With an absent-minded gaze
And spectacles of clearest glass
Is sitting at the foot of a wall
At the foot of a wall facing a wall

He says I'm going to count from one to a hundred
At a hundred I'll be through
Once for good   once for all
I start in   *One, two* and so on

But at 73 he is not quite sure
It's like trying to count the strokes of midnight
    and making them only eleven
It's pitch dark   how can you tell
You try to rebuild the rhythm from the intervals
But when did it begin?

And you wait for the next hour to strike

He says come on   we've got to finish
Let's start all over   once again
Once and for all
One to a hundred
One. . . .

[AUTREFOIS]

Once I made poems
That followed the whole radiant line
From centre to circumference and beyond
As if there were no circumference   only a centre
And as if I were the sun: all around me limitless space

This is to make the elemental force flash all along the radiant
To gain prodigious meteoric speed—
What central pull can then hinder our escape
What heavenly concave dome keep us from piercing it
When we have power to burst into the infinite?

But we learn the earth is not flat
But a sphere, and the centre's only focus
Is at the centre
And we learn the length of the radiant line, that too well
    travelled road
And soon we know the surface of the globe
Measured inspected surveyed   an old
Well-beaten track

And then the weary task
Of pushing the perimeter to its bounds
Hoping to find a crack in the surface of the globe
Hoping to burst the boundaries
And find once more the liberty of light and air.

58

Alas soon comes despair
The strength of all that radiant line becomes
This still point on the surface

Just like a man
Who taking too short a road, dreading his destination,
Shortens his stride and so defers his goal,
I must learn subtlety
Must infinitely divide the infinitesimal distance
Between chord and arc
To create a space a little like what is beyond
And find in it a hiding-place
A reason for my life and art.

59

SENTRY-GO

We said, Let there be night
Just for a doubtful little star.
Have we the right to decree night
Night on the world and on our heart
Just for a spark?
Will it shine
In the enormous desert of the sky?

We said, Let there be night
For our own sake
Let night run loose on the earth
Well knowing what it is
What animal it is
We have learned what wilderness
Its passing spreads before our eyes

We have said, Let night loose on the earth
Well knowing what it is
And will make our lonely sentry-go
Just for a star   still unsafe unsteady
Which may be only a shooting star
Or even the false phantom glimmer
In the vault that our famished eyes
Hollow out within us.

7. Sans titre

You thought that all was quiet
All spent
You thought this little death was easy

But no, you knew I was afraid
Dared make no move
Hear nothing
Say nothing
Lest I wake entirely
And I closed my obstinate eyes
Like one who cannot sleep
Stuffing my ears against the pillow
Trembling lest sleep should leave me

Already I felt sleep withdrawing
The way an open door in winter
Lets the soft warmth out
And into the room
Admits the cold which shakes you from your torpor
Scourging you
Making you as keenly conscient as steel

And now

Wide-open eyes too carnally open-eyed and flooded
Survey the pilgrimage
Of eyes mouths hair
This light   too vibrant
Stripping this pallor
From the autumn sky

63

And my gaze goes madly hunting
This splendour disappearing
This clarity escaping
Through the holes of time

Autumn almost stripped
Of the moving gold
Of the woods
And then this sunset
Sliding over the horizon's edge
Making me cry out in anguish

All these things that are being taken from me

Sorrow, I listen to your breaking wave
To the shimmer of voices and the wind
A symphony already lost already melting
In a trembling air which slips into the past
My eyes my heart   my open hands
Hands under my eyes   these splayed fingers
Can hold nothing
Can only tremble
In the terror of their emptiness

Now my whole being wide awake
Is as if unrolled over an immense expanse
Having no further refuge in itself
From the deadly shuddering of the winds
And my sensual heart is open like a wound
Pouring out in torrents of desire
My blood sprayed to the four corners of the sky.

64

[QU'EST-CE QU'ON PEUT]

What can we do for our friend
Down there
An arm's-length away

What can we do for our friend
Whose suffering has no end

What can we do for our heart
With its torment and its smart

What can we do for our heart
When it sets forth all alone

And we see it from where we stand—
This child who is going to sea

From the cliff's edge where we stand—
A child whom a ship is taking

A ship that the sea is taking
On a voyage to the wind's end

A voyage in sunny weather
But already the sea is pounding

And the surf is beating harder
And the journey meets the storm

And as the whole sea thunders
And the wind wails in the rigging

The ship has turned to a groan
And the child to a thing of torment

And from the cliff where we stand
Our gaze is on the sea

And our arms hang at our sides
Like a pair of useless oars

Our gaze grieves on the sea
Like great compassionate hands

Two poor hands doing nothing
Knowing all, doing nothing

What can we do for this heart of ours
This child on a voyage all alone
Torn by the sea before our eyes?

66

A LITTLE ENDING OF THE WORLD

Oh! Oh!
The dead
birds

The birds
the doves
our hands

What has become of them
that they are strangers now

Once they could be seen
meeting in brightness
hovering in the sky
brushing each other with such pleasure and talking
so tenderly

What has struck them down
four hands that sing no more
here lying dead
abandoned

I had a foretaste of the world's end
and your face seemed to die
before this silence of four doves
before the death of these four hands
    Fallen
in a row side by side

And we ask
    of this bereavement
what secret death
what secret work of death
by what deep tunnelling through our darkness
that our glances did not wish to plumb
    did death
devour the life of the birds
shoot down the song and break the flight
of four doves
laid out under our eyes

so that they are now without a pulse
and with no radiance in their being.

68

SALUTATION

Only that I may love you
May see you
And be in love with seeing you

Oh not to speak to you
For no interchange
                    no converse
One thing surrendered, another withheld
For no such half-bestowals of ourselves

But only to know you are
To love this: that you are.

Only that I may love you
I welcome you
Into the airy valley of my thought
Where you walk alone and without me
Entirely free

Heaven knows you will be heedless there
And open only to the sun
And wholly intent upon your flowering
With no dissembling in your play

You will be shining and alone
Like a flower beneath the sky
Without one petalled folding-in
One quiver of exquisite modesty

69

I am alone, I too
Circling the valley
I am the watchful hill
Circling the valley
Where the gazelle of your grace will spring
In the confidence and clarity of that air

Alone too I will have the joy
Before my eyes
Of your perfect motions
Of the perfect stances
Of your solitude

And heaven knows you will go again
As you have come
And I shall have you no more

I'll be perhaps no less alone
But the valley will be a desert then
And who will speak to me of you?

70

[CAGE D'OISEAU]

I am the cage of a bird
A cage of bone
Holding a bird

The bird within his cage of bone
This is death who makes his nest

Whenever everything is still
You hear the fluttering of his wings

And after laughing heartily
If you break off suddenly
You hear a cooing sound
Deep down
Like a little funeral bell

That is the bird in prison there
Death inside my cage of bone

If he'd like to fly away
Is it you who'll make him stay
Is it I
Who can say?

He'll not go until he has
Eaten everything there is
My heart
The spring of blood
With life inside

And carry my soul off in his beak.

8. Escort

I walk beside a joy
A joy that is not mine
A joy of mine that is not mine to enjoy

I walk beside that joyful I
I hear his joyous step sound at my side
But cannot change place with him on the pavement
I cannot put my feet in his steps and say
                              See, this is I!

This escort is all I need for the moment
But in secret I am plotting an exchange
Through all kinds of discoveries, alchemies
Transfusions of the blood
Rearrangements of atoms, conjuring tricks

So that some day, transposed,
I shall be borne along by the dance of those joyous steps
With the sound of my own feet dwindling away beside me
And the loss of their aimless steps as they fade away
Under the feet of a stranger turning down a side-street.

75

LES SOLITUDES

Attente

MY HOUSE

I want my house with open doors
An open house for all the poor.

I'll open it to all who come
As one who can himself recall
How long he suffered out of doors
Beset by all the dead
Refused at every door
Bitten by cold, eaten by hope

By endless weariness worn out
By dogged hope made desperate

Forever seeking after grace
Forever on the trail of sin.

79

WEARINESS

I am no longer one of those that give
But one that must be healed.
And who will enter into my misery?
Who'll have the courage to embrace
This half-dead life?
Who'll find me under so much ash
And blow upon it and revive the spark?
And carry me out of myself
Far away, oh far, far!
Who'll hear me now, who have no voice
As I wait?
What woman's hands will lay upon my brow
The gentleness that gives us sleep?
What woman's eyes into the depths of mine
Will care to go, proud and searching
Into the hollows of my darkened eyes,
And hope to pass and not be soiled,
What woman's or what kindly eyes
Can wish to go down to this cell
And rake together and revive,
And recapture and retain
The spark that's hardly there?
What voice can echo back,
What voice of pity
Clear with the transparency of crystal
And all the warmth of tenderness,
Rouse me to love, and bring me happiness again,
Rouse me to God's presence in the universe?
What voice can make its way, softly and with no pain
Into my inner silence?

Jeux

What am I doing hanging to this rope
This rope, a star suspended by its light alone,
Shall I die hanging here
Or die like a drowned man weary of his shipwreck
Who slips into the all-embracing sea
That true sister who embraces us
Transposes the light as we descend
And holds it against our eyes, filling them full

Remember the sea that cradled you
Old deadman swung to the soundings of the lead,
Companioned by green light,
Disturbing with your wash the order of her motion
Over the beds of the unnumbered waves,
And now stroked by seaweed in the quiet depths
Remember the waves and how they cradled you
Old deadman buried in silence undersea.

83

[JE ME SENS BALANCER]

I feel I am swaying on a tree-top
No, you women's voices you will not break
The purity of my song
And though you have made, my friends of yesterday,
The stifling heat where I would fall asleep
Tonight I have found upon this height
Among the leaves murmuring like a wave
A refuge in the bright air of my hope
Life in the memory of coolness.

84

BAIGNEUSE

O morning of my eyes on the water!
A luminous bathing-girl has drawn upon herself
    all the light of the landscape.

85

THE FLUTE

So close to what is felt:
The breath is there, the flute marries it,
So closely,
Wholly against the breath.

86

[ALLEZ-VOUS ME QUITTER]

Are you about to leave me   you   all my voices
Am I about to lose you each and all
The symphony and every word
Shall my heart be as if you had never been
This emptiness that keeps no count
That cannot hold what is?

87

[LA GRANDE VOIX]

The great voice of the wind
A whole commingled voice from far away
Then increasing as it comes
                    becomes
This voice   that voice
Out of this tree   that other tree
And keeps on and becomes once more
A great confused voice from far away.

88

Pouvoirs de la parole

As for you, pass by the tower
Reach your hand to the tower's top
And sign to those who cannot see inside.

Keep that silence and make those signs
So the world shall know of things within the tower
That something lives inside, not to be seen
But existing, like a precious pearl.

SILENCE

All words are becoming inward things for me
And my mouth is closed like a coffer holding treasures
No longer uttering these temporal words, these words of
    passage,
But closing and keeping its words like a treasure, its words
Out of the reach of time that soils, of time that passes,
Its words which are not of time
But image time in the eternal,
A sort of images
Not of whatever is passing by
But a sort of symbols
A sort of evidence of eternity passing by

Things unique, unspeakable,
Passing here among us the living,
Forever nevermore,
And my mouth is closed like the lid of a coffer
On the things which my soul keeps to itself,
Which it keeps
Incommunicable
Possessing them elsewhere.

[PAROLE SUR MA LEVRE]

Words on my lips now take your flight
    you are no longer mine
Go strangers and my enemies already:
Among all these closed doors, be closed yourself
     in your unopening marble.

Having no power upon you since your birth

I am in conflict with you now
As with any alien thing
And find in you no friendly tremor
As in the friendly flesh that moulds itself to mine
And marries my shifting form as well.
Already you are among the impassable things

      that ring me round
One of the barriers made to stifle me.

93

[TE VOILA VERBE]

Behold you, words that face my self
                a poem facing me
Through a projection from beyond me
          from my under-consciousness
An unexpected and unwanted son
A being hard to recognize, brother, enemy.
And there is the poem, an emptiness closing around me
With the hunger of its terrible will to live,
Closing upon me with its deadly tentacles,
Each word a sucking mouth, a leech that clings to me
Seeking to swell itself with my blood.

I shall feed these trials with my marrow.

EACH AND ALL

Each and all, all and each, interchangeable things
A pair of words
Symbols
Of the unutterable identity
Where the whole poem can assume the light

Nature, you have sung me
The duet of two ambiguous voices,
A bodiless balancing
Beyond the opacity of Number
Flux and reflux of a single flood, O merging flood,
Waves reborn forever
Only to throw out and unroll
Light to the limits of the shore

You this word, and you that
Oh make yourselves more than a common flesh
For the love of my soul that married you.

Each and all reversible
And often I could do nothing for this alteration
But couple you together.

95

[JE SORS VOUS DECOUVRIR]

I am going forth to find you elsewhere, poets
Each of you somewhere else beyond this little life
I will go find you in the life of everyone
And in the death of everyone
Where they have strewed their life's flight on the floor
Not in my house, ah no.

There, out there, you shall awake
Convulsing all my universe
Before me and building it again
In an overflowing of every form and frame.

96

MUSIC

Music afar from me tonight
Unveiled afar you carry my spirit there
Song of the hills   rhythms
That distance draws together in these sprays
A bouquet from the reclining countryside.

Do not the children hear this all day long
And the angels,
These landscapes drawn all into one blaze of light?

You speak to me words I have never heard,
Upheavals of the heart,
Infinite cradlings of my rising hopes,
Abortive loves wrapped in a gesture
And which desire has barely brought to flower in my eyes

And the barely begun departures for far-off lands
Smiles given the unknown

Or tears   you so long sought
Tears to be drunk   heart's intoxicating liquor
Welling within
Brimming this heart that falls in ruins
Aspects to be adored

And these rages. . . .

Let me receive you as a mistress
You will make my torture divine
And make this love, dead as my land,
Blossom as it unrolls under the motionless sun
Of a day which the hours have not devoured,
You will give blood to these memories
That are already blurring
Or that remain within the room in the depth
Of this my still deconsecrated heart
Where so many dews have fallen without a flower
And you, so many flowers with no heart at your corolla
And so many corollas already all too faded
Who died in the midst of these liquid breathings
Poured for your thirst upon the evening air
And amid this slaking in the cool of dawn

Here you are mine between my hands, those two deserving
    souls of my body,
Eternally my own in your passage
Through these hands of mine, these seekers after tenderness
And which nothing has filled to fullness
These things requiring utter plenitudes,
Hands which are not happy.

These sad hands, see, these empty things
Craving, athirst, desirous hands
Whom I am bidding be silent tonight,
                  saying it is not you,
You hands of pallid flesh
Which shall possess me.

You are transforming this abused desire,
Scattered in dust to all the winds of day,
To what here seizes and takes possession of my life
My inaccessible life and my too-distant soul

Here takes possession of them turned at last to flowers. . . .

99

[UN POEME A MIJOTE]

A poem has been hatching all day long
And has not come
Its presence has been felt all day long
                          buoyant
Like a spring that bubbles up
And seeks an outlet
But this one has been lost in the earth
There is nothing now.

We walked all day as madmen do
In a presentiment of balance
In a prevision of some light to come
Like madmen all at once aware
Of something disentangling in their brain
Of a sort of light that wishes to be born
As if they were going to recover what they lack
But they are maddened by the day's slowness to be born
And see, how the glimmer disappears again
Goes back into the sun and out of sight
And the door of darkness shuts again
On a solitude more incomprehensible
In the way that a single note, persistent, strident,
Annihilates the whole world.

100

La parole de la chair

LAMPS

Old
Poor lights hung
Motionless in the smoke
Like lost silences
What are you doing here, and what,
I ask, are you looking at?
Lost dead lights

Sadness   like you of the ready-made smiles
And the glances around
Like you   hanging
On the swinging breasts of the dancing-girls
Red and green and blue
As poor as you are
As old
As dead.

103

[AU MOMENT QU'ON A FAIT LA FLEUR]

In the instant when we have brought to flower
All of our love enclosed within that flower
When weariness suddenly withers it between our fingers
When weariness suddenly rises all around
To advance upon us like an enclosing circle,
The unexpected enemy advances
And begins by abolishing the world outside us
Abolishing the world as it approaches us
Comes to abolish the flower between our hands
Where our love was immersed and blossoming,
Oh then our love so dispossessed withdraws within us
Flows back on us and takes us unawares
Fills us to bursting with a flood past bearing
Strikes us down with an unexpected frenzy
And we are terrified
And as if disarmed before this utterance
Before the sadness of this utterance of the flesh
We had not expected and which strikes us like a blow
                                         in the face.

104

[A PART VINT-CINQ FLEURS]

Forget those 25 flowers burnt away
    all day long the garden has been beautiful
Apart from 25 flowers that have withered—
    and we are setting forth on a pleasant walk
    as if nothing were wanting
But we feel
Despite the cool of the unveiling evening
    and the perfect airy cadence of our steps
The weight of those dead flowers stealing upon us
And stealing upon us
25 flowers fallen in a corner of the garden
Which make the whole garden topple within us
Which make the whole garden turn over within us
Putting the garden in convulsion.

105

[ON DIRAIT QUE SA VOIX]

It is as if his voice were cracked
Already?
Sometimes he captures that old burst of laughter
But when he is tired
The sound does not fill his form
It's like a voice in a boiler
This sound that stops in the middle
As if he swallowed the end of it already uttered
It breaks and does not reach out to the air
It stops
       and it's as if it ought not to have begun
As if nothing were true

I who used to believe that all was true at such a moment
Already?
Then what can ail him that he goes on living
And why has he not gone away?

106

[APRES LES PLUS VIEUX VERTIGES]

After the oldest of the vertigoes
After the longest of declines
And the slowest poisons
One day at noon
Your bed as certain as the tomb
To our bodies fainting on the sands
Yawned like the sea.

After the slowest of approaches
The fieriest of caresses
After your body a pillar
Bright and consummately hard
My body a river outspread and pure to the water's edge.

Between us the ineffable happiness
Of distance

After the brightness of the marble
The first movements of our cries
And suddenly the weight of the blood
Foundered within us like a shipwreck
The weight of the fire fell on our perished hearts

After the final sigh
And the fire had crossed the shadow on the ground
The cables of our arms are cast off for a mortal journey
The bonds of our embraces fall of themselves and go adrift
    on our bed

Stretching out now like a desert
And all the inhabitants are dead
And our perished eyes see nothing more
Our eyes blinded by the pupils of desire
As our love vanished like an unbearable shadow
And we felt our isolation rising like an impassable wall.

Under the red sky of my eyelids
The mountains
Are companions of my arms
And the forests burning in the darkness
And the wild beasts
Passing with the claws of your fingers
O my teeth
And the whole earth dying in a vise

Then blood covering the earth
And the secrets burnt alive
And all the mysteries torn to pieces
Night was delivered in our final cry

It was then she came
Again and again
It was then she passed through me
Again and again
Bearing my heart upon her head
Like an urn that kept its radiance.

[LEUR COEUR EST AILLEURS]

Their hearts have gone elsewhere
To heaven perhaps
And in the meantime they are wandering here
My heart has gone forth among other stars
Far from here
And ploughs the night with a cry I do not hear
What drama is perhaps being played out far away?
   I do not wish to know
I would rather be a dead young man laid out
Would rather have abandoned everything.

With the vault of heaven for hat
The earth for steed
It behoves us now to know
What journey we shall make

I would rather have lost everything
Would rather be a dead young man laid out
Under a silent vault
In the night-light's long unflickering flame
Or perhaps in the depths of the sea
In a failing greenish glow
For an age of time without hours or tomorrows,
Beautiful dead maidens, calm and sighing
Will slip their alien forms into my eyes

After they've kissed my mouth without a cry
And followed the dreams of my hands
Over the serene curves of their shoulders and their loins
After the voiceless company of their tenderness
Once having seen their shapes come without hope
I'll see their shadows vanish without pain. . . .

Accompagnement

MY SOLITUDE HAS BEEN IMPURE

My solitude at the fall of night
It was not pure
My solitude   it was not tender
At the day's end at the edge of night
Like a soul we follow expecting nothing
Knowing her for a sister.

My solitude was not good
Like her we followed
(Expecting nothing) and had chosen
To be an all-unbending bride
For the homestead of our life
For the coffin of our death
That guardian of our silent bones
From which our soul is breaking free.

My solitude on the edge of night
Was not that friend
Was not the company of that guardian angel
The clear depth of that well
The withdrawn circle of a love
Where the heart binds and unbinds itself
At the centre of our waiting.

Like a madness it took us by surprise
Like water welling up
And seeping in
Through the cracks in our carcass
Through all the holes in our substantial self
Inadequately fleshed
And which the worms of our putrefaction
Leave open.

113

She came   an infidelity
Like a girl of the streets
Whom we followed
Only to leave
She came to ravish and abandon us.
In the circle of our treachery
She came to rob us
To leave us crippled
She came to sever us

So then of the soul in such distress:
It is our self which is disjoined
It was myself whom I deserted
It is my soul which takes this cruel walk
Stark naked in the icy desert
As I fall alone into this possession
Into this narrow solitude
So that I may take no part in the terrible game
At the bidding of all those little irreplaceable
Seconds.

And what shadow at the edge of things
What luminous friendly shade
Waits on the steps of our panic flight?
She whom no mercy followed
Not even our own.

[MES PAUPIERES EN SE LEVANT]

My eyelids lifting have left my eyes empty
Left my eyes open to an enormous solitude
And the servants of my eyes have not gone forth
My conscious looks have not gone forth like gleaners
Around their little world
To gather heavy sheaves of things
They bring nothing to people my barrenness
And it is as if they had lived inside me
And their door had never been unclosed.

115

[UNE SORT DE REPOS]

A kind of rest
looking at a passing sky

All that weighs on us was put aside
Despair   noiseless   sleeps under the rain

Poetry is a goddess
we have had report of her

Her body too pure for our heart
Sleeps all arrayed
As luck would have it she is turned away
We'll not go now
To steal from her those jewels
She does not wear when she is naked.

116

ANOTHER ICARUS

It's out of the wind it's in the wind
It's only a hole we make in our passage through it
A knot we tie in the fleeting thread of time

And well we know that across this slender thread we've made,
Across these shaky stations built on the journey of our going,
There is only a cry toward the depths that are forever
There is only a cry
                    from a place that lasts forever
Where the stems of the fruits are already broken
And all the stalks of the flowers and petals of the flowers
    are devoured
Where these feather-wings of our waxen soul have already
    melted
Only feathers in the wind feathers floating on the wind
With no home port.

117

[LE BLEU DU CIEL]

The blue of the sky and the light flowing within us
    had served us all day long for hope
But we had always the secret and abiding fear
    of this return to the port of desolation
Which we have reached now despite the beauty
    of the night above us
Withdrawn from the open sea, from our rest on the sea,
    from all our journeys on the bright and enormous sea
But we know not what counter-current at our back
    takes us again with a desperate obstinacy
And carries us back to the batterings of this maelstrom
Which lets us rise to the surface just when we were
    at last about to perish.

118

[L'AVENIR NOUS MET EN RETARD]

The future puts us in arrears
Tomorrow is like yesterday we cannot touch it
With our life before us like a ball chained to our heels
The wind at our back crushes our forehead against the air

    We use ourselves up step by step
    We use our steps up one by one
    We use ourselves up in our steps
    It's what is called taking useless steps

Here is the earth beneath our feet
Flat as a great table
Only we do not see where it ends
(This is because our eyes are weak)

Nor do we see its underside
Through force of habit
And this is a pity
For highly important things are settled there
Relating to our feet and footsteps

It is there that geometrical confabulations take place
With us for their centre and locus

It is there that the sequence of points becomes a line
A string attached to us
And there the game becomes a terribly pure game
With a relentless constancy in its march-to-the-end
                    which forms the circle
    This prison.

Your feet walk on a stubborn surface
On a surface that bears you like an emperor

But your steps fall through into the void
                                pointless steps

They make a circle
                       and it is a point
We put them here and there, anywhere,
                              through twenty interlacing streets
And we hear toc-toc on the sidewalk
                         always in the same place
There, beneath your feet

The pointless steps fall under us into the void
   and we think we'll never meet with them again
We think the pointless step is something given once and
   for all
   lost once and for all
But it's only a funny way of sowing things
And has its law
The footsteps form a circle and look ironically at you
The prisoner of pointless steps.

120

Dans ma main le bout cassé
de tous les chemins

WORLD BEYOND RECALL

In my hand
The shattered stump of all the roads

When did we let the moorings slip
How did we miss the roads

Insuperable space between
Bridges broken
Roads lost

On the sky's edge a hundred faces
Impossible to see
The light cut off long since
A great knife of darkness
Cuts across my eyes

In this place of disaffection
Any appeal of outstretched arms
Is lost in the insuperable air

The memory we question
Has heavy curtains at its windows
Why ask it anything at all?
The shadow of the absent ones is voiceless
Is melting now into the walls
Of the empty room.

Where are the bridges the roads the doors
The words do not come
The voice fails to carry

Am I to spring out on this tenuous wire
On a wire of make-believe strung over the gulf
Perhaps to find the faces turned away
And batter myself with a heavy hollow blow
Against their absence

Bridges broken
Roads cut
The beginning of all presence
The end of the wedge of all fellowship
Lies broken in my hand.

[UN BON COUP DE GUILLOTINE]

One good stroke of the guillotine
To emphasize the space between

I put my head on the mantelpiece
And the rest goes about its work

My feet go where they have to go
My hands their little business do

On the slab of the mantelpiece
My head has an air of holiday

A smile is on my lips
As if I were but newly born
My gaze is sent forth, calm and clear
Like a soul saved and released

It is as if I'd lost my memory
And this has made my head a pretty fool's.

125

[IDENTITE]

1

Identity
Always broken

The knot has begun to feel
The twistings of the rope of which it's made

2

The strange pace of our heart
Comes back to us through the fog
We hear it
            what a funny clock

A room with furniture
The clock on the mantelpiece
They are all part of the room
You look out of the window
You go and sit at your desk
You work
You rest
All is quiet

All at once: tick-tock
The clock comes plucking at your ears
Plaguing you through the road of your ears
It comes with its tiny blows
To break the room in pieces

You raise your eyes: the shadows have shifted the chimney
The shadows are pushing the chimney around
The furniture is all changed

And just when everything began to live on its own
Each strange piece
Has begun to contradict another one

Where is one to stay
To live?
Everything is in holes and pieces.

[FIGURES A NOS YEUX]

Face before our eyes
Faces scarcely
Arisen
And which have not yet left the darkness
What desire is drawing you
To pierce the darkness
And what darkness draws you back
You faces evanescent to our eyes?

Faces hovering
At the borders of the visible and rising
In a game which veils you and unveils you
You come here to die on the edge of an imaginary smile
And to enfold us in the warmth of your gravity
In a hovering between appearance and farewell
You leave us and your eyes will not have seen us
But we shall have fallen into you as into the night.

128

[LE DIABLE, POUR MA DAMNATION]

The Evil One, for my damnation,
Has let me look behind the scene
Through the opening in the curtain.
He has, in playing so with me,
Lifted the corner of the veil
Concealing life. Oh, not for long!
Only enough to let me grasp
What's lying on the other side
And to whet and quicken
Curiosity,
That thirst which drowned our mother Eve
In sin.
Just enough to catch a glimpse
Of the enchantment of the night,
The splendour of eternal day,
The astonishing reality,
Just enough for me to hear
The choir of birds and fairies
The universal harmony
Of these colours and these songs.

And I remain there in the theatre
Eyes wide open, ears pricked up,
Famished, devoured by expectancy
And by the despair that mounts within me,
Parched by thirst and by this watch kept
    on the gap in the curtains, asking myself "Is this the
    moment? See, the curtains are about to part! I am about
    to see, I am about to hear!
I am going to lay my eyes on life!
A tremor is running along the curtains:

They are going to open! Look, look!
    it will last only a fraction of a second, only as long as a
    smile, a sob, a leap!
Now is the time! The curtain is stirring!"
But no, nothing. Perhaps a draught of air,
A breath of air along the surface!
And then, afterward, when this has gone on really too long,
    when there's no end to this closure, when one's worn out
    with waiting,
I say to my heart, "No, come on now,
You know it's all a hoax,
A trap, a joke,
See now, look at us, we're dying here,
Come along, heart, let's be going!"
But at the moment when my heart succumbs,
When it has no more strength to resist,
When it is sick, drained of blood,
At the moment when it's filled with the hunger to be healed,
    to go forth, to breathe,
To soften, to submit,
Look, the damned curtains
Are opening,
Letting us see
Once more the day, once more the night,
And letting the song escape like a sickness beginning, a
    dawn which is barely breaking
A light which is gathering
A beautiful outline which is forming,
                        sketch of a dance

. . . .

What ecstasy! We are drunken,
My heart and I, we are mad!
    And we remain in the hall
Though the curtain has fallen.
And we gaze hungrily
At the opening that is closed,
At the dropped curtain.
"Will it open soon? Tomorrow?"
And the Evil One repeats this trick
    a hundred times.
I hear him laughing in the wings,
Savouring our death by this slow fire,
    watching the madness rising in the depth
    of our widened eyes
He knows we are his dupes,
This is his pleasure.
We know it too indeed, but will not quite believe it because
    then we would have to surrender
And go away
Just as the veil was perhaps about to be
    raised in a moment, and forever!

131

Voyage au bout du monde

Ships rocked in the harbour
Gently rocked by memories of travel

And then we find the memories wandering alone
    and coming back to find no harbour.
Memories with no home port
Find the port deserted
A great empty place with no ships at all.

135

[JE REGARDE EN CE MOMENT]

I look at the sea this moment and see a wheeling of birds
Circling some memory of a vanished vessel's masts
That were once their home port on the sea

And at this moment I have also seen in flight
A phantom ship with two deserted masts
That the birds did not see, did not recognize
So in the sky and on the sea remains
A wheeling of birds with no port for a home.

136

[MON DESSEIN]

I do not plan to rear a handsome building
> vast, solid and perfect
But rather to go forth in the open air

There where the plants are, air and birds
There where the light is and the reeds
There where the water is.
In water and air and on the earth there are
All kinds of things and animals
We need not name them, there are too many
But each of us knows there are so many and so many more
And each is different and unique
You do not see the same ray of light
Falling twice in the same way on the same water
From the spring

Each is singular and alone

I take one here
I take one there
And put them together so they may keep each other company
This is not the end of the night
This is not the end of the world!
It is myself!

137

[IL NOUS EST ARRIVE DES AVENTURES]

Adventures have come to us from the world's end
When you come from afar it is not to remain there
(When you come from afar it was because you had to leave)
Our glances are tired of being swept by the same trees
By the saw against the sky of the same trees
And our arms of sweeping at the same place forever.
Our feet no longer fixed us there to the earth
They were drawing our bodies to days beyond our sight.

Imperative departures have been ours
From the first departure of all and thence unendingly
Beyond our sight and into a horizon of renewals
Which is only this appeal from afar that shapes the landscape
Or that cliff-like barrier
Which lashes the rage of our desire to know
And whose weight winds up within us
The spring of our salvation

We have not had too many snows to eat
We have not had too many winds and storms to drink
We have not had too much ice to carry
Nor too many dead to carry upon our icy hands

There are those who could not leave
Who dared not wish to leave
Who had no joy in their eyes with which to kiss the spaces
Who had no lightnings of blood in their arms to open them
They fell asleep on the benches
Their souls were stolen from them while they slept
They awoke with a start like those servants
Whom the master surprises at their idleness

138

We, we had no desire to stop
We had not too much weariness to conquer
For the franchise of our gestures into space
For the freedom of our eyes on every place
For the free bounding of our hearts over the hills

And there are those who did not wish to go
Who wished not to go but to stay

We look at them and shrug our shoulders
We are not of the same race.

They have awakened, these animals in the pen
Who spend their soulless ardour in the brothels
And return to a mindless sleep
They have awakened, these book-keepers, busybodies,
Devourers of neighbours, classifiers of sins,
Collectors of taxes, inchmeal assassins,
Eaters of souls, the well pleased, the prudent,
Arse-kissers, bootlickers, bowers and scrapers,
Who renounce longwindedly and with perfect composure,
Having nothing to renounce.

This is a country of little creatures to be stepped on
You cannot see them because they're dead
But you'd like to boot them in the bum
And see them underground for the sake of the beauty of
    unpeopled space.

The others, we are the wild ones, we are the all-alone
In our heads there is only the thought of embracing
We have only the taste for going forth, the taste like
    a hunger
We are already where we are no longer
We have no business here
We have nothing to say and we hear no voice of any friend.

140

[BOUT DU MONDE!]

The world's end! The world's end! It's not so far!
We thought in our heart it was an endless journey
But we discover the flatness of the earth
The earth that image of ourself
And now here is the world's end itself
We have to stop
We have arrived

Now we must find out how to make the pilgrimage
And how to return, with backward steps, from where we
    have come
And how to return, against the current, from our illusion
Not turning our head toward the new voices of our riches—
We have already waited too long, pausing all alone
We have already lost too much heart in pausing.

We huddle around the emptiness of what we do not have
The one acceptable reality of what we might have had
Colonies and possessions and a whole belt of islands
Things made in their likeness and sparked here in the
    absolute centre of what we do not have
Which is what we desire.

141

[A PROPOS DE CET ENFANT]

With reference to this child who didn't want to die
And whose likeness at least we cherished
like a framed picture in the drawing-room
We could have been wildly mistaken about him
Perhaps he was not made for the high priesthood as we had
    thought
Perhaps he was only a child like any other child
And only high beside our lowliness
And only luminous beside our darkness—
                                with nothing at all
(Let's bury him, picture-frame and all).

He has led us here like a squirrel that loses us in the woods
And our care and cunning were wasted in scanning the
    underbrush

Our eyes were tired of trying to mark his leap in the
    underbrush

And so our whole soul has been fooled as it lay in ambush
for his deceitful passage
We thought to find a whole new world by the light of his
    eyes
We thought he would lead us back to the lost paradise.

But now let's bury him, or the frame and the likeness at
    least,
And all the abortive paths we beat as we pursued him
And all the inviting traps we laid to catch him.

[C'EN FUT UNE DE PASSAGE]

She was a passer-by within our world
For a weekend   an hour
                what does the period matter
For a visit to our world
                our city our kind of world

Indeed she is a queen with every right to live
Her visit gave us pleasure
                despite our fear of the living
When she came it might have hurt our eyes a little
But it was good for our eyes

She said to us, let me visit you
She did not know us as we were
But as her desire and curiosity saw us

She said to us, let me visit your world
So then we took her by the hand
A little awkwardly because we were not used to her
And because her step was not in step with ours
We are a little too used to the pace of our own steps
Queens put us a little out of step. . . .

143

[IL VIENT UNE BELLE ENFANT]

She came a lovely child to lay new eyes on us
"We'll let you look upon our land of coffins
It's not a pretty country but we'll take you round it.
We are a little surprised by your coming.
                    We were expecting nothing more."
"No, I don't want to, better the meadows in the light."
"We would die in the light, you must not think of it.
                    It can't be done."
"Then I would rather go away. . . ."

144

INVENTORY

This child, they said,
$\qquad$ had not the destiny that was required of him
He came into the world under unfavourable conditions
Among horrible animals of whom the worst
$\qquad$ were not wild beasts
Who might have devoured him in his infancy
$\qquad$ for his own good. . .
But there are always those who devour and alter nothing.

145

La Nuit

And now, when was it we devoured our joy?
All other questions have now locked up the lips
of their thirst
And this one only is heard in its persistence and its pain
Like a distant memory tearing us till now
This bridal pledge and kind of parley with a bride
And now that we've torn this furrow in ourselves
Now we have come so far
This question comes again
Filling us with the voice of its despair—
When was it we devoured our joy
Where was it we devoured our joy
Who was it who devoured our joy?
For there is surely a traitor among us
Who took his place at our table when we sat down
such as we are
And as we were

All those who died in this kind of caravan that went by
All of that day's children and good animals who died
And all those who, heavy-footed now, keep on their way
With clenched jaws within this kind of dream
And in this kind of desert of a final drought
And in this light now gone behind an impassable
and pointless wall of emptiness
Among all of us who sat down such as we were
and as we are
(For we carry the weight of the dead more than that
of the living)
Who is it among us who devoured our joy
Where nothing is left but this kind of memory
which has torn us in these pieces?

148

Who is it whom each of us sheltered among us
Welcomed among us
Entertained among us in a kind of secret understanding
This treacherous brother we took for a brother
    and carried on our journey of fellowship
And guarded in the conspiration of fellowship
And followed here, where our joy has been utterly devoured
Carelessly   beneath our eyes
Where nothing is left but this kind of memory
    which has torn us in these pieces
And this despair on the deathbed of its illusions.

149

[ON N'AVAIT PAS FINI]

I

We had not done with that fooling of ourselves
We were still moving on and losing sight of ourselves
We had not done with finding out our wounds
We had not done with failure to control ourselves
Desire was redescending on us like a fire

Our unseen shadow is continuous
It does not leave us to fall on the road behind
We carry it hanging on our shoulders
It is dogged in its pursuit of us
Devouring, with every step that we advance,
The light of our personal day

We cannot put it from us
Turning around we suddenly find it there
We cannot shake it from us
And when it is almost under us at noon
It is still making underneath our feet
A terrible hole in the light.

150

2

We were all together in the midst of time
We had drawn together in the midst of space
O farther from paradise than we used to be
We were all met together for a mighty festival
And we asked of God the Father and of Jesus Christ
And of the Holy Ghost who is the Third Distinction
We asked of them to open Paradise a little
To lean out and look down
And see if they could recognize the world a little
And if it looked a little like their idea of it
And if their work was not wholly admirable

Those who came with a soul from the good God
Having eyes from the good God
To make a pure alliance with the world

151

3

The earth was in darkness and devouring its sins
The love of kind was like the savage beasts'
The flesh was howling like a damned soul
And the blows against us and the blows between us
Resounded in the deafness of thickening time

Here are those who came with their spirit fetched from God
Here are those who came with the morning in their eyes
Their eyes were opened upon us like a dawn.
See how their love has wholly washed our flesh
They have made of all the earth a flowering meadow
A field of flowers for the visitation of the light
Of flowers for the presence of everything under heaven
They have drunk the whole earth like a wave
They have eaten the whole earth with their eyes
They have found again the lost voices gone astray
They have gathered up all the words which had been
                                         fooled away

152

4

Time treads upon our heels
In the shadow we make upon the road
All those of us   time and the shadow have come upon us
They have nibbled our life away at our heels
And see, how men go grinding themselves away
The steps of their passage lost without return
The loveliest presences devoured
The purest blooms effaced
And we seem to hear behind us the steps of the evening
Coming to strip us of all our friendships
Coming to efface and encircle all of them
Coming to unpeople the earth before our eyes
To drive us back like the Flood to a rocky height
To dispossess us of the whole universe
And take us in the trap of being alone for always

But see, how those have come whom we awaited
See, they have come with their spirits fetched from God
They have come with the nets of their hands
With the marvellous snare of their eyes for nets
They have come from behind time and the shadow
On the heels of time and the shadow
They have gathered up everything we had let fall.

153

5

There is no true comfort when the night comes on
No way to quiet ourselves or be relieved
To look around us with a smile
And feel we are free because we no longer see the shadow

It is only because we no longer see it
Its presence is no longer clothed in light
And we are only a little cloistered light
Because it has given its hand to all the shadows
A little inner presence in the enormous void
And the appeal of our eyes finds no echo
In the silence of the empty shadow

We are going a journey to the sun
Ours is a passage clothed in light
With our shadow at our heels like a horse
Devouring our death as we go on

With our shadow at our heels like an emptiness
Drinking our light as we go on

With an emptiness at our heels like a trench
A hole in the light upon the road
Swallowing our passage like oblivion.

154

WEIGHTS AND MEASURES

It's not a matter of tearing things up by the hair
Of tying a woman's hair to a horses's tail
Of piling up the dead all helter-skelter
Put to the sword, the edge of time.

We can amuse ourselves making knots out of parallel lines
It's quite a metaphysical diversion
The absurd not being reduced to the fact of Cyrano's nose,
But looking at the absurd with our heads upside down
We catch glimmerings of other worlds
We see cracks in our world which turn to holes

We can be sorry to see holes in our world
We can be shocked by holes in stockings, waistcoats,
                            holes in gloves where a finger shows
We can insist that all of it be mended

But a hole in our world is something more indeed
Provided we catch a foot in it and let our heads
Fall into it and ourselves fall into it head first
This lets us wander about and even return
This can free us to measure the world on foot,
                            foot by foot.

155

La Mort grandissante

And until the broken sleep whose wandering shadow
                    circles and will not take me
Blurs everything, leaving only that point in me
                    heavy heavy heavy
Which awaits the waking at morning to draw itself upright
At the centre of me the destroyed, bewildered,
                    crippled, in agony.

158

[AH! CE N'EST PAS LA PEINE]

Oh the pain of living is not worth while
When we can die of it so well
Not worth while living
And seeing them dying, dying
The sun and stars

Oh it is not worth while to live
And to outlive the flowers
And to outlive the fire in our ashes
But so much worthier to die
With the flower in our heart
With this glowing
Flower of fire in our heart.

159

[C'EST EUX QUI M'ONT TUE]

It is they who have killed me
Struck me in the back with their weapons, who killed me
Struck me to the heart with their hatred, who killed me
Struck on my nerves with their howling, who killed me

It is they in their avalanche who have crushed me
Splintered me like a log of wood

Snapped my nerves like a cable of iron wire cut short
When all the threads in a wild bouquet
Spring out and curl back in quivering points

Who crumbled my body like dry bread
Picked my heart to pieces like a crust
Scattered it all into the night

They have trodden it all down without even seeming to
Without knowing or wanting to know or being able to know
Without thinking, without caring
Only by their terrible mysterious strangerhood
Because they did not come to me to embrace me

Oh into what wilderness we must go
To die quietly by ourselves.

[MAIS LES VIVANTS]

No, the living have no pity on the dead
And what would the dead do with the pity of the living
For the heart of the living is hard as a living tree
                        and they go their strong and vivid way
Though the heart of the dead lies bleeding
                        and stricken with grief
And all a prey to blows, too open to blows
                        with its uncovered carcass
For the living going their way have no pity on the dead
Who remain with their hearts uncovered to the wind.

161

[NOUS AVONS MIS A MORT]

"We have put pity to death
We cannot let her live
We are the proud
We deny the gaze of pity."

"We are the gaze of pity
We cannot cease to live on earth
The gaze of pity."

STILL ANOTHER
or
THE DYING ONE
WHO CLINGS AND COVERS ME WITH ASHES

There is certainly someone who is dying
I had meant to pay him no attention
                        to let the corpse fall by the way
But it is the way now that is losing way
                        and he is I
This dying man who moulds himself to me.

We had thought that suffering
Would mould our faces to the splendid hardness of our bones
To the clear and resolute silence of our bones
That last unconquerable castle of our being,
Would stretch clearly over our bones the skin of our faces
The tired and troubled flesh of our faces
Continually crumpled and convulsed
The skin which hangs in the wind the tawdry flag of our face

A feeble flag to all the winds which betray us—
That suffering would reduce it to the fixed form of
    our clear bones.

But was suffering forestalled
Could death have made a secret nest in our very bones
Pierced, debased our very bones
Chosen to make its home in the very marrow of our bones
Amidst our bones?
So that after filtering through all our flesh
Through all the layers of flesh given it to feed on
After all that gnawing at the soft and sluggish flesh,
Suffering itself should find no substance to lay hold on
Nothing of substance to be firmly seized
Nothing solid to pierce with a living sting
No living silence to heat white hot
No core of silent feeling to torture without destroying
But only meet with a surface in decay
A porous fabric dissolving
A phantom which crumbles and leaves nothing but dust.

163

We shades of corpses as those shades are realities of corpses,
    bones of corpses
And what pity (and what wonder) seizes us
    sentient shades of corpses
And what kindred terror
Facing this answer given
This proffered likeness
Bones of corpses.

When we are reduced to our bones
Resting upon our bones
in bed with our bones
with the night before us

We shall unjoint our limbs
                    and set them in a row for listing
To see what is lacking
To find the joint that is out of joint
For it is unthinkable to sit
                    quietly accepting
                    the body of this death.

For always standing within us
A man not to be beaten down
Erect within us, turning his back
                    to where our looks are turned
Erect in his bones, eyes fixed on the void
In a fearful dogged facing and defiance.

Have done with the hill which you shall never climb
And the cloak covering the silence of the bones
And the living grape of the heart at last despairing
Wherein this cross might now be carved in grain
Instead of the acid blade of scorn,
In the place where the driven knife is fixed
Whose handle probes the ever-aching wound
Whenever you turn your hand toward your breast
There where the cross is carved with its iron arms
Like the iron wire nailed to the tree's bark
Cutting the surface, but this is a wound
The scarring bark soon covers and enrinds
And in time the iron thread which cuts the surface
Is seen embedded in the core of the trunk—
So let the cross be planted in your heart
And your head and arms and feet stretched far beyond
And Christ over all and our small sufferings.

Have done with the hill which lies beyond the horizon
Henceforward take your place at the edge of things
With the whole land behind your shoulders
And nothing before you but this march to make
With the pole marked out by a measurable hope
And your heart drawn by the lodestone cross of iron.

My heart this heavy stone within me
Heart turned to stone by this barren fixity
And backward gazing at the fires of the city
And hunger lingering in the ashes of regret
And spent regrets for all the possible lands

Gather your cloak about you hopeless pilgrim
Gather your cloak about your bones
Fold those arms unhinged by happiness relinquished

Pull the cloak of your poverty over your bones
And as for the dried grape seeded in your heart
Now let its skin be softened by another

Have done with the hill unthinkable in the scheme
Of an absurd land where you yourself were only
An ambush laid for the secret learned by night,
The secret of the illusion of escape from grief.

166

S'endormir a coeur ouvert

And I will entreat thee of thy grace to crucify me
And nail my feet to thy holy mountain
So that they may not run upon forbidden roads
The roads that lead bewilderingly away
From thee
And that my arms should also be held wide open
To love by firm-fixed nails, and that my hands
My hands drunken with flesh, burning with sin,
Should be, beneath thy gaze, washed in thy light
And I will entreat thy love, a fiery chain,
To bind me fast beside thy calvary
And keep my gaze ever upon thy face
While still above thy suffering shall shine out
The resurrection and the light eternal.

169

[APRES TANT ET TANT DE FATIGUE]

After ah so much of weariness
The hope of sleeping like a child

At last at last a better rest
After all the sinful sleep
Holy rest invites us now

Tonight to coolness of the sheets
To whiteness of the pillow, to
The abandon of the night

To the bliss of going to sleep
With a heart already freed
With a soul already soothed

Wretch bewildered by
The happiness of going to sleep.

No more the furious plunge into the black
No more the end of courage
No more death in a mirage
Despair

My misery is wiped away
But who was it that came to me
And how made me anew

That I this very night should find
The confidence and warmth again
To fall asleep like a bird
To be a child and fall asleep
In the coolness of his bed
In that protective happiness
Which launches two into the dark?

Who has made me new again
Holy Virgin, that my shoes
Quietly rest beneath my bed?

Who has but so recently
And so simply brought me back
Every false step blotted out
To seek my bed so simply now
In this place to be a child
Sleeping soft, confidingly

Sleeping with an open heart
Tender leaves above, around

To go off to sleep
In music of sleep
In waves which penetrate—
Innocent and simple as
One would go to heaven.

171

[LES CILS DES ARBRES]

The eyelashes of the trees edging this great eye of night
Tree-eyelashes edging this great night-eye
The mountains of the shores around this great quiet lake
                             the sky   the night
With all our roads at rest now in their hollows
Our fields in their holy stations
                        with scarcely the passing tremor
of the breeze in the grass
With our fields quietly unrolled
          on this brown warm and cool depth of the earth
And our forests have let down their hair over the slopes. . . .

172

INTRODUCTION

REGARDS ET JEUX DANS L'ESPACE

POUVOIRS DE LA PAROLE

LA PAROLE DE LA CHAIR

ACCOMPAGNEMENT

DANS MA MAIN LE BOUT CASSE DE TOUS LES CHEMINS